Dear
BLACK GIRL,

You Are More Than Enough!

*Twenty affirmations that will have you believing in,
appreciating, and loving yourself!*

Brittany Allen

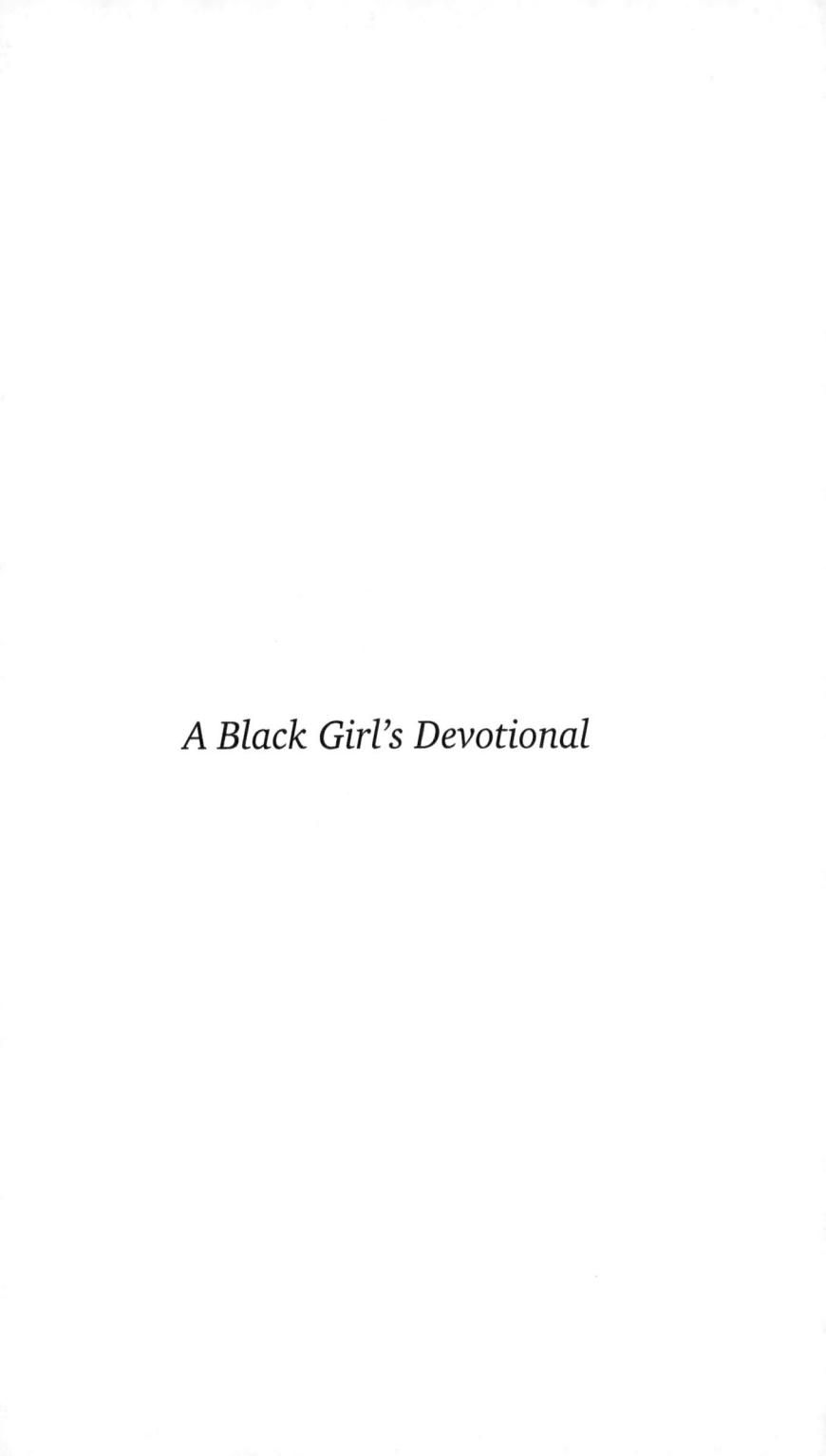

A Black Girl's Devotional

TO MY FAMILY:

Thank you for always believing in me!

CONTENTS

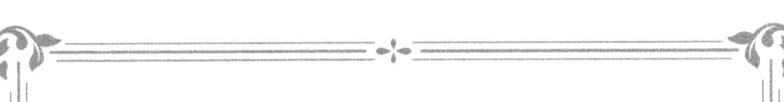

PREFACE

I faced adversity as a young African American female in the corporate world. I began my career in human resources at age 22, shortly after graduating from the wonderful Fayetteville State University (Bronco Pride!). I knew I had a long road ahead of me and wished I had these affirmations to encourage me at the start of my career.

I landed great jobs in human resources and had good leaders in my corner. Still, life wasn't always so peachy as an African American female in the workplace. I always showed up to work every day, giving 110%, because I understood that if I wanted that promotion, that recognition, and that respect, I had to work ten times harder than my colleagues. Two of my dear friends often told me, "You are light years ahead of your age," simply because I put in the work. Have you ever felt like your best was never enough? Like you had to work ten times harder than others to prove yourself? As if you were unappreciated in life, in the workplace, etc.? I am certain that there are thousands of girls like me, so I wrote this book for YOU and US.

Black girl, I hope these affirmations remind you daily that YOU ARE MORE THAN ENOUGH! Never stop believing in yourself! Take this book, look in the mirror, and repeat after me: I'm MORE THAN ENOUGH!

AFFIRMATIONS

I AM STRONG

I will not let anyone undermine my strengths. I will wake up every day with the mindset that I am better than I was the day before. I will tackle today with positivity and throw all negativity out the window. Because of my strength, I will conquer the day!

Dear Black girl, you have superpowers. Now use them.

Bible verse: 2 Corinthians 12:10

"That's why I take pleasure in my weaknesses, and in the insults, hardships, persecutions, and troubles that I suffer for Christ. For when I am weak, then I am strong."

I AM SMART

I take pride in my work, knowing my thoughts and ideas are creative and brilliant. My knowledge is worth millions, and I will let it flow freely today. My brain is a powerful tool, and I will use it to my advantage. Today, I will brighten the room that I walk into with my intelligence!

Dear Black girl, your brain is your weapon. Make great use of it.

Bible verse: Proverbs 2:6

"For the LORD grants wisdom! From his mouth come knowledge and understanding."

I AM BEAUTIFUL

The color of my skin does not define what I can achieve. My melanin is stunning. My melanin is gorgeous. I was made in God's image, and therefore, I am perfect. My lips are luscious; my skin is bright; my eyes are glowing; my hair is perfectly laid; my mind is beautiful; I am flawless!

Dear Black girl, you're beautiful. Just take a look in the mirror so that you can see for yourself.

Bible verse: Song of Solomon 4:7

"You are altogether beautiful, my darling, beautiful in every way."

I AM COURAGEOUS

I am ready to face the challenges that today may bring. I am not afraid, for I know that God is with me. I will use my voice and always stand up for what is right.

Dear Black girl, your bravery is omnipotent. Stand tall!

Bible verse: Deuteronomy 31:6

"So be strong and courageous! Do not be afraid and do not panic before them. For the LORD your God will personally go ahead of you. He will neither fail you nor abandon you."

I AM BLESSED

My blessings overflow. The land that I step on is blessed. I am grateful for my career, my home, my clothes, my shoes, and the food that I eat. I have so many blessings that I cannot begin to count them one by one. Thank you, God, for every blessing.

Dear Black girl, I pray that your blessings exceed what you could imagine. Grab your gifts and never let them go!

Bible verse: 2 Corinthians 9:8

"And God will generously provide all you need. Then you will always have everything you need and plenty left over to share with others."

I AM WORTHY

I deserve all of the good that comes my way and more. I deserve recognition and appreciation. The qualities that I possess are far beyond valuable. I am a precious jewel.

Dear Black girl, polish your crown and show up today. You are worthy!

Bible verse: 1 Peter 2:9

"But you are not like that, for you are a chosen people. You are royal priests, a holy nation, God's very own possession. As a result, you can show others the goodness of God, for he called you out of the darkness into his wonderful light."

I AM TALENTED

I have the skills and knowledge to perform my job and greatly assist others. My gifts are so diverse that they can be used in many ways. I will use the gifts that God has given me in ways that glorify him today.

Dear Black girl, you have gifts. Share them with the world!

Bible verse: Romans 12:6

"In His grace, God has given us different gifts for doing certain things well. So if God has given you the ability to prophesy, speak out with as much faith as God has given you."

I AM CALM

I will remain undisturbed, no matter today's difficulties or the days to come. Hurtful words will not come from my mouth when I face negativity. I will not be hateful towards others, even if they slay me. I will not worry or wonder about what today may bring. God, please grant me a spirit of serenity.

Dear Black girl, you are not angry and loud. Your situation will not alter your attitude. Choose peace!

Bible verse: Philippians 4:6-7

"Don't worry about anything; instead, pray about everything. Tell God what you need, and thank him for all he has done. Then you will experience God's peace, which exceeds anything we can understand. His peace will guard your hearts and minds as you live in Christ Jesus."

I AM CONFIDENT

I know who I am. I value myself, and I am powerful enough to institute change. I am comfortable in my skin. I speak with confidence, I walk with confidence, and I am confident in my abilities.

Dear Black girl, you can do anything you put your mind to!

Bible verse: Hebrews 13:6

"So we can say with confidence, "The LORD is my helper, so I will have no fear. What can mere people do to me?"

I AM HUMAN

I am allowed to make mistakes. I am allowed to try repeatedly. I must give myself grace. Today, I will take the opportunity to learn something new.

Dear Black girl, keep going and keep trying!

Bible verse: Genesis 1:27

"So God created human beings in his own image. In the image of God he created them; male and female he created them."

I AM A LEADER

I teach, listen, motivate, and serve. I make good choices, realizing that my decisions impact others. I lead with empathy and integrity. My light shines so brightly that others choose to follow. I am an unselfish leader.

Dear Black girl, you are the head and not the tail. You are a fierce leader.

Bible verse: Jeremiah 1:5

"I knew you before I formed you in your mother's womb. Before you were born I set you apart and appointed you as my prophet to the nations."

I AM LOVED

I have family and friends in my corner who think the world of me. I am a joy to be around. I receive the love that is all around me.

Dear Black girl, you are very much loved!

Bible verse: 1 John 4:7-8

"Dear friends, let us love one another, for love comes from God. Everyone who loves has been born of God and knows God. Whoever does not love does not know God, because God is love."

I AM RESPECTED

I treat myself with the utmost respect because I deserve it. I deserve kindness. I treat others how I expect to be treated. I accept myself fully, flaws and imperfections.

Dear Black girl, what you give is what you receive. Give and earn respect!

Bible verse: 1 Peter 2:17

"Respect everyone, and love the family of believers. Fear God, and respect the king."

I AM UNIQUE

I am special in my own way. My looks, talents, and skills are all different. This makes me stand out among others. I appreciate my uniqueness. Because I am unique, I am valuable.

Dear Black girl, you are fearfully and wonderfully made!

Bible verse: Isaiah 64:8

"And yet, O LORD, you are our Father. We are the clay, and you are the potter. We all are formed by your hand."

I AM SUCCESSFUL

I will achieve my goals and dreams. I believe that I can do anything. I am the best at what I do. I am prepared to receive the new opportunities that will be offered to me today.

Dear Black girl, you are succeeding in life! Keep it up!

Bible verse: Genesis 39:2-4

"The Lord was with Joseph, so he succeeded in everything he did as he served in the home of his Egyptian master. Potiphar noticed this and realized that the Lord was with Joseph, giving him success in everything he did. This pleased Potiphar, so he soon made Joseph his personal attendant. He put him in charge of his entire household and everything he owned."

I AM UNAPOLOGETIC

I am authentic. I accept myself. I own the good, the bad, the pretty, and the ugly because they are all part of my story. I will live out loud and love every piece of me.

Dear Black girl, be yourself and unapologetic for it!

Bible verse: Isaiah 50:7

"Because the Sovereign LORD helps me, I will not be disgraced. Therefore, I have set my face like a stone, determined to do his will. And I know that I will not be put to shame."

I AM HEALTHY

I am grateful for my body. My image is perfect; I put good things into my body to maintain my healthiest version. I am full of energy and life.

Dear Black girl, your body is your temple, explicitly created by God. Take care of it!

Bible verse: 3 John 1:2

"Dear friend, I hope all is well with you and that you are as healthy in body as you are strong in spirit."

I AM UNSTOPPABLE

I can do anything. Today, I will soar like an eagle with wings. I am determined; I will accomplish all tasks set forth for me. I cannot be tamed.

Dear Black girl, no limits, no boundaries. Soar!

Bible verse: Proverbs 24:16

"The godly may trip seven times, but they will get up again. But one disaster is enough to overthrow the wicked."

I DESERVE

I work hard and earn all things that I receive. I deserve good things. I deserve a great life, career, love, and appreciation. I deserve happiness.

Dear Black girl, you deserve the best because you are the best!

Bible verse: 1 Corinthians 15:10

"But whatever I am now, it is all because God poured out his special favor on me—and not without results. For I have worked harder than any of the other apostles; yet it was not I but God who was working through me by his grace."

I AM MORE THAN ENOUGH

I am worthy of all the good things that life has to offer. Self-doubt does not live here; I do not need validation from others or to prove myself. I will live on my terms, accept compliments, and surround myself with positive energy. I am secure and proud of who I am.

Dear Black girl, you are and will ALWAYS BE MORE THAN ENOUGH!

Bible verse: Psalms 139:13–14

"You made all the delicate, inner parts of my body and knit me together in my mother's womb. Thank you for making me so wonderfully complex! Your workmanship is marvelous—how well I know it."

CREATE YOUR OWN
AFFIRMATIONS

I AM _____

_____
_____
_____
_____
_____
_____
_____
_____
_____

Bible verse: _____

_____
_____
_____
_____
_____
_____
_____

I AM _____

_____
_____
_____
_____
_____
_____
_____
_____
_____

Bible verse: _____

_____
_____
_____
_____
_____
_____
_____

I AM _____

_____
_____
_____
_____
_____
_____
_____
_____
_____
_____

Bible verse: _____

_____
_____
_____
_____
_____
_____
_____

I AM _____

_____
_____
_____
_____
_____
_____
_____
_____
_____

Bible verse: _____

_____
_____
_____
_____
_____
_____
_____
_____

I AM _____

_____
_____
_____
_____
_____
_____
_____
_____
_____
_____

Bible verse: _____

_____
_____
_____
_____
_____
_____
_____

www.ingramcontent.com/pod-product-compliance
Lightning Source LLC
Chambersburg PA
CBHW060357130626
46553CB00003B/1278